Published simultaneously in 1994 by Exley Publications in
Great Britain and Exley Giftbooks in the USA.
Second printing 1994.

Selection and arrangement © Helen Exley 1994.
ISBN 1-85015-433-3

Edited by Helen Exley.
Text researched by Margaret Montgomery.
Designed by Pinpoint Design Company.
Pictures researched by P. A. Goldberg and J. M. Clift / Image
Select, London.
Typeset by Delta, Watford.
Printed and bound in Hungary.
Exley Publications Ltd, 16 Chalk Hill, Watford, Herts WD1 4BN, United Kingdom
Exley Giftbooks, 232 Madison Avenue, Suite 1206, NY 10016, USA

Acknowledgements: Pepita Aris: extract from "Introducing Spanish Food" from
Bergh's International Annual Digest of Gastronomy '93/94, Bergh Publishing, 1993;
Shashi Deshpande, Germaine Greer, Benoîte Groult, Attia Hosain, Kathy Lette,
Antonia Till: extracts from *Loaves & Wishes*, edited by Antonia Till, Virago, 1993;
Keith Floyd: extracts from *Floyd on France*, BBC Books 1987.
Exley Publications is very grateful to the following individuals and organizations for
permission to reproduce their pictures: Archiv Für Kunst (AKG), Art Resource (AR),
The Bridgeman Art Library (BAL), Chris Beetles (CB), Christie's Images (CI), Fine
Art Photographic Library (FAP), Popperfoto (Pop), Scala (Sc). Cover: (FAP)
Guiseppe Magni, Anthony Mitchell Paintings, Nottingham; Page 5 (title page): (BAL)
Eloise Harriet Stannard, Christopher Wood Galleries, London; Page 6: (AR) Claude
Monet; Page 8: (BAL) Victor Gabriel Gilbert, Giraudon, Musée des Beaux-Arts,
Rouen; Page 10: (BAL) Mark Gertler, Connaught Brown, London; Page 12: (FAP)
Fanny Fildes, Gavin Graham Collection; Page 15: (FAP) Alfred Augustus
Glendening; Page 17: (CB) Loucy Willis, Private Collection; Page 19: (FAP) C.V.M.
Desliens; Page 20/21: (BAL) Arthur Hughes, Maidstone Museum and Art Gallery,
Kent; Page 22: (BAL) Frederick Daniel Hardy, York City Art Gallery; Page 24: (FAP)
Gabriel-Germain Joncherie, Gavin Graham Collection; Page 27: (Sc) Pieter Bruegel
the Younger, Museum voor Schone Kunsten, Gent; Page 28: (BAL) Jan Havicksz
Steen, Belvoir Castle, Leicestershire; Page 31: (CI) Edouard Frere; Page 33: (BAL)
Frederick McCubbin, National Gallery of Victoria, Melbourne; Page 35: (BAL)
Robert Furber, Victoria & Albert Museum, London; Page 37: (AR) © DACs 1994,
Chaim Soutine (1894-1943), "The Little Pastry Cook", Orangerie, Paris; Page 39:
(CB) Loucy Willis, Private Collection; Page 40: (AKG) Anna Archer, Copenhagen;
Page 43: (FAP) William Hough; Page 45: (BAL) © 1994 Walter R.I. Tyndale (1856-
1943), "Miss Lydiard's Stall, Bath" (detail); Chris Beetles Ltd., London; Page 47:
(BAL) © 1994 Helen Schjerfbeck (1862-1846) "The Bakery", Pohjanmaan Museum,
Oslo; Page 49: (BAL) J. Kynnersley Kirby, Gavin Graham Gallery, London; Page 51:
(AKG) William Pape; Page 53: (BAL) Marcel Rieder, Gavin Graham Gallery, London;
Page 54/55: (BAL) Frederick George Cotman, Walker Art Gallery, Liverpool; Page
56: (AKG) Turkish Bookplate, 16th Century, Artist Unknown; Page 59: (CI)
Peter Ilstred; Page 61: (BAL) © 1994 Ditz, "Biscuit Baking Day" (detail).

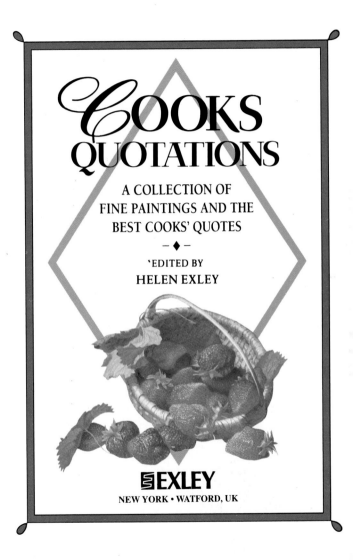

COOKS QUOTATIONS

A COLLECTION OF
FINE PAINTINGS AND THE
BEST COOKS' QUOTES

– ◆ –

'EDITED BY
HELEN EXLEY

▤ EXLEY
NEW YORK • WATFORD, UK

COOKING AS AN ART

"Cookery is not chemistry. It is an art.
It requires instinct and taste rather
than exact measurements."

MARCEL BOULESTIN,
from "Petits et grands plats"

– ◆ –

"I feel a recipe is only a theme, which an
intelligent cook can play each time
with a variation."

MADAME BENOIT

– ◆ –

"Some people like to paint pictures, or do
gardening, or build a boat in the basement.
Other people get a tremendous pleasure out of
the kitchen, because cooking is just as creative
and imaginative an activity as drawing,
or wood carving, or music."

JULIA CHILD

– ◆ –

WHAT MAKES A GOOD COOK?

"What does cookery mean? It means the knowledge of Medea and of Circe, and of Calypso, and Sheba. It means knowledge of all herbs, and fruits, and balms and spices.... It means the economy of your great-grandmother and the science of modern chemistry, and French art, and Arabian hospitality. It means, in fine, that you are to see imperatively that everyone has something nice to eat."

JOHN RUSKIN (1819-1900)

– ◆ –

"Even more than long hours in the kitchen, fine meals require ingenious organization and experience which is a pleasure to acquire."

ELIZABETH DAVID (1914-1992),
from "French Country Cooking"

– ◆ –

GREAT INGREDIENTS

"It was in France that I first learned about food. And that even the selection of a perfect pear, a ripe piece of brie, the freshest butter, the highest quality cream, were as important as the way the dish you were going to be served was actually cooked."

ROBERT CARRIER

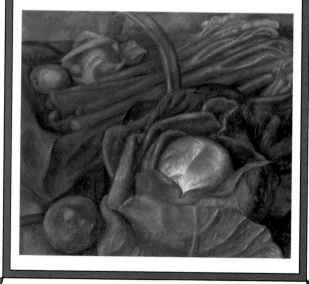

"Watch a French housewife as she makes her way slowly along the loaded stalls...searching for the peak of ripeness and flavour....
What you are seeing is a true artist at work, patiently assembling all the materials of her craft, just as the painter squeezes the oil colours onto his palette ready to create a masterpiece."

KEITH FLOYD,
from "Floyd on France"

— ◆ —

"This [Spanish food] is real food, village food – direct, simple and tasty. The recipes are suggested by the flavours, textures and colours of the ingredients themselves, and are not distorted by decoration or artifice in any way....
No se admiten trampas en la cocina, the Spaniards would say – no tricks to disguise indifferent food in the kitchen."

PEPITA ARIS,
from "Bergh's International Annual Digest of Gastronomy '93/94"

— ◆ —

FROM THE HEART

"Happy and successful cooking doesn't rely only on know-how; it comes from the heart, makes great demands on the palate and needs enthusiasm and a deep love of food to bring it to life."

GEORGES BLANC,
from "Ma Cuisine des Saisons"

— ♦ —

"The secret of good cooking is first, having a love of it.... If you're convinced cooking is drudgery, you're never going to be good at it, and you might as well warm up something frozen."

JAMES BEARD

— ♦ —

"The most indispensable ingredient of all good home cooking: love for those you are cooking for."

SOPHIA LOREN, b.1934

— ♦ —

CENTRAL TO LIFE ITSELF

"We must eat to live and live to eat."

HENRY FIELDING (1707-1754)

— ♦ —

"Pleasures may be divided into six classes, to wit, food, drink, clothes, sex, scent and sound. Of these, the oldest and most consequential is food: for food is the body's stay, and the means of preserving life. No other pleasure can be enjoyed, unless a man has good health, to which food is ancillary."

MUHAMMED IBN AL-HASSAN IBN MUHAMMED IBN AL-KARIM
AL KATIB EL-BAGHDADI (13th Century)

— ♦ —

"Food...can look beautiful, taste exquisite, smell wonderful, make people feel good, bring them together, inspire romantic feelings.... At its most basic, it is fuel for a hungry machine;...."

ROSAMOND RICHARDSON

— ♦ —

SIMPLICITY

"In cooking, as in all the arts, simplicity is
the sign of perfection."
CURNONSKY

— ◆ —

"A crust eaten in peace is better than a banquet
partaken in anxiety."
AESOP

— ◆ —

"Cuisine is when things taste like themselves."
CURNONSKY

— ◆ —

"If pale beans bubble for you in a red
earthenware pot
You can oft decline the dinners of
sumptuous hosts."
MARTIAL (A.D.41-104)

— ◆ —

"I detest...anything over-cooked, over-herbed, over-sauced, over elaborate. Nothing can go very far wrong at table as long as there is honest bread, butter, olive oil, a generous spirit, lively appetites and attention to what we are eating."

SYBILLE BEDFORD

– ♦ –

LIFE'S GREAT PLEASURE

"If a man be sensible and one fine morning, while he is lying in bed, count at the tips of his fingers how many things in this life truly will give him enjoyment, invariably he will find food is the first one."

LIN YUTANG (1895-1976)

– ♦ –

"Show me another pleasure like dinner which comes every day and lasts an hour."

TALLEYRAND (1754-1838)

– ♦ –

"...food is, delightfully, an area of licensed sensuality, of physical delight which will, with luck and enduring tastebuds, last our life long."

ANTONIA TILL,
from "Loaves & Wishes"

– ♦ –

" A home is a place where a pot of fresh soup simmers gently on the hob, filling the kitchen with soft aromas...and filling your heart, and later your tummy, with joy."

KEITH FLOYD

GOOD COOKING COMES FIRST

"One cannot live well, love well or sleep well
unless one has dined well."

VIRGINIA WOOLF (1882-1941),
from "A Room of One's Own"

– ◆ –

"When we no longer have good cooking in the
world, we will have no literature, nor high and
sharp intelligence, nor friendly gatherings,
nor social harmony."

MARIE-ANTOINE CARÊME

– ◆ –

We may live without poetry, music and art;
We may live without conscience, and live
without heart;
We may live without friends, we may live
without books;
But civilized man cannot live without cooks.

OWEN MEREDITH (EDWARD R. BULWER-LYTTON) (1831-1891)

– ◆ –

Those who are one in food are one in life.
MALAGASY SAYING

– ♦ –

"We must keep these pleasures in proper
perspective; we must indulge them reasonably,
not grossly....
The savour of good food and good wine
is one of the elements of true civilization,
and no man who embarks upon a fine meal
in that knowledge can rise from it
without thinking something real has been
added to his nature."
BERNARD LEVIN

– ♦ –

"Bad men live to eat and drink, whereas
good men eat and drink in order
to live."
SOCRATES (469-399 B.C.)

– ♦ –

THE MOST VITAL INGREDIENT

A smiling face is half the meal.

LATVIAN PROVERB

— ◆ —

"...planning a brilliant menu and preparing it
beautifully doesn't guarantee a recipe for
success. It's pointless giving painstaking thought
to food, if you haven't given food to *thought*.
The truth is, people are the most
important ingredient."

KATHY LETTE,
from "Loaves & Wishes"

— ◆ —

"The same food may be consumed in a happy
or an unhappy atmosphere, but only in the
first will it be a feast."

MARGARET WILLES,
from "Soop Meagre and Syllabub"

— ◆ —

BAD, BAD COOKS

"She did not so much cook as assassinate food."

STORM JAMESON (MARGARET) (1891-1986)

— ♦ —

"Dinner at the Huntercombes' possessed only two dramatic features – the wine was a farce and the food a tragedy."

ANTHONY POWELL, b.1905

— ♦ —

"Too many cooks may spoil the broth, but it only takes one to burn it."

MADELEINE BINGHAM,
from "The Bad Cook's Guide"

— ♦ —

Hostess, at the end of a totally inadequate meal:
"I do hope you will dine with us again soon."
Alfred Hitchcock: "By all means.
Let's start now."

MEMORIES OF CHILDHOOD

"We all have hometown appetites.
Every other person is a bundle of longing
for the simplicities of good taste once
enjoyed on the farm or in the hometown
[he or she] left behind."

CLEMENTINE PADDLEFORD

— ♦ —

"When from a long distant past nothing
subsists, after the people are dead, after the
things are broken and scattered, still, alone,
more fragile, but with more vitality, more
unsubstantial, more persistent, more faithful,
the smell and taste of things remain poised for a
long time, like souls, ready to remind us,
waiting and hoping for their moment, amid the
ruins of all the rest; and bear unfaltering...the
vast structure of recollection."

MARCEL PROUST (1871-1922)

— ♦ —

SLAVES IN THE KITCHEN

"Who inu hell," I said to myself, "wants to try
to make pies like Mother makes when it's so
much simpler to let Mother make um inu
first place?"
HARIETTE ARNOW

$-\blacklozenge-$

"Throughout the world it is the women who
bear the responsibility for feeding their families.
In countries devastated by drought and
deforestation it is the women – and sometimes
the children – who spend up to seven hours a
day just gathering the firewood or water. And
that is before the picking, cleaning, sorting,
grinding, pounding, preparing and cooking...."
ANTONIA TILL

$-\blacklozenge-$

"This kitchen closed because of illness – sick
of cooking."
REFRIGERATOR MAGNET

"There has always been a food processor in the kitchen. But once upon a time she was usually called the missus, or Mom."
SUE BERKMAN

– ◆ –

"Miss, Mrs., Ms., and I'm still in the kitchen."
REFRIGERATOR MAGNET

– ◆ –

MAKE MEMORABLE MEALS

"I used to love the way everyone talked about
food as if it were one of the most important
things in life.
And, of course, it is.
Without it we would die. Each of us eats
about one thousand meals each year.
It is my belief that we should try
and make as many of these meals as we
can truly memorable."
ROBERT CARRIER

– ♦ –

"Life is so brief that we should not glance either
too far backwards or forwards...therefore study
how to fix our happiness in our glass and
in our plate."
GRIMOD DE LA REYNIÈRE

– ♦ –

WITH ABANDON!

"Cooking is like love. It should be entered into with abandon or not at all."

HARRIET VAN HORNE, b.1920,
from "Vogue", October 1956

– ◆ –

"Serve the dinner backward, do anything – but for goodness sake, do something weird."

ELSA MAXWELL,
from the New York "Herald Tribune", 1963

– ◆ –

"The qualities of an exceptional cook are akin to those of a successful tightrope walker: an abiding passion for the task, courage to go out on a limb and an impeccable sense of balance."

BRYAN MILLER,
from "The New York Times", February 23, 1983

– ◆ –

SIMPLY DELICIOUS

"O, blackberry tart, with berries as big as your thumb, purple and black, and thick with juice, and a crust to endear them that will go to cream in your mouth, and both passing down with such a taste that will make you close your eyes and wish you might live forever in the wideness of that rich moment."

RICHARD LLEWELLYN (1907-1983)

– ♦ –

"My tongue is smiling."

ABIGAIL TRILLIN, aged four,
after eating chocolate ice-cream, from "Alice, Let's Eat"

– ♦ –

"Huge blond *babas, Mont Blancs* snowy with whipped cream, cakes speckled with white almonds and green pistachio nuts, hillocks of chocolate-covered pastry...."

GIUSEPPE DI LAMPEDUSA,
from "The Leopard"

"A KIND OF TEMPLE"

"My kitchen is a mystical place, a kind of temple for me. It is a place where the surfaces seem to have significance, where the sounds and odors carry meaning that transfers from the past and bridges to the future."

PEARL BAILEY, b.1918, from "Sanctuary"

– ♦ –

"I was taught from childhood of the sanctity of food. Not a piece of bread could be thrown away without kissing it and raising it to one's eyes as with all things holy."

ATTIA HOSAIN, from "Loaves & Wishes"

– ♦ –

"Sir, Respect Your Dinner: idolize it, enjoy it properly. You will be many hours in the week, many weeks in the year, and many years in your life happier if you do."

WILLIAM MAKEPEACE THACKERAY (1811-1863)

– ♦ –

TOO FANCY

"Much of what I read and see [about food] is so perfect, so fancy that it defies imitation – anyway, for most ordinary mortals. The foodie movement has put cookery on a pedestal when cookery is for the kitchen, the family and friends. Pedestals are for prima donnas, heroes and, perhaps, a handful of chefs. But cookery is for every day."

KIT CHAPMAN

– ♦ –

"Life is too short to stuff a mushroom."

SHIRLEY CONRAN, b.1932,
from "Superwoman"

– ♦ –

"'Cuisine heureuse', which consists of marrying natural products with one another,...is the antithesis of cooking to impress."

ROGER VERGE

– ♦ –

"But some of us are beginning to pull well away, in our irritation, from...the exquisite tasters, the vintage snobs, the three-star Michelin gourmets.

There is, we feel, a decent area somewhere between boiled carrots and Beluga caviare, sour plonk and Chateau Lafitte, where we can take care of our gullets and bellies without worshipping them."

J.B. PRIESTLEY (1894-1984)

— ♦ —

ABUNDANCE

He from forth the closet brought a heap
Of candied apple, quince, and plum, and gourd;
With jellies soother than the creamy curd,
And lucent syrops, tinct with cinnamon;
Manna and dates, in argosy transferr'd
From Fez; and spicèd dainties, every one,
From silken Samarcand to cedar'd Lebanon.

JOHN KEATS (1795-1821)

— ♦ —

"The near end of the street was rather dark and had mostly vegetable shops. Abundance of vegetables – piles of white and green fennel, like celery, and great sheaves of young, purplish, sea-dust-coloured artichokes...long strings of dried figs, mountains of big oranges, scarlet large peppers, a large slice of pumpkin, a great mass of colours and vegetable freshnesses...."

D.H. LAWRENCE (1885-1930)

— ♦ —

THE "MIRACLE OF BREAD"

"Bread is the warmest, kindest of words.
Write it always with a capital letter, like
your own name."

RUSSIAN CAFÉ SIGN

– ♦ –

Why has our poetry eschewed
The rapture and response of food?
What hymns are sung and praises said
For the home-made miracle of bread?

LOUIS UNTERMEYER

– ♦ –

"The peasants of Sicily, who have kept their own
wheat and make their own natural brown bread,
ah, it is amazing how fresh and sweet and clean
their loaf seems, so perfumed, as home-made
bread used all to be before the war."

D.H. LAWRENCE (1885-1930),
from "Sea and Sardinia"

– ♦ –

DANGER!

"I've run more risk eating my way across the country than in all my driving."
DUNCAN HINES

– ♦ –

"People are the only animals who eat themselves to death."
AMERICAN MEDICAL ASSOCIATION ADVERTISEMENT

– ♦ –

Epicures dig their graves with their teeth.
TAMIL PROVERB

– ♦ –

"Indigestion: A disease which the patient and his friends frequently mistake for deep religious conviction and concern for the salvation of mankind. As the...Man of the Western Wild put it, with, it must be confessed, a certain force: 'Plenty well, no pray; big belly ache, heap God'."
AMBROSE BIERCE (1842-?1914)

MOUTH-WATERING DAY-DREAMS

"...I would stand transfixed before the windows
of the confectioners' shops, fascinated by the
luminous sparkle of candied fruits, the cloudy
lustre of jellies, the kaleidoscopic inflorescence
of acidulated fruitdrops...."

SIMONE DE BEAUVOIR (1908-1986)

– ◆ –

"He lay back for a little in his bed thinking
about the smells of food...of the intoxicating
breath of bakeries and the dullness of buns....
He planned dinners, of enchanting aromatic
foods...endless dinners, in which one could
alternate flavour with flavour from
sunset to dawn without satiety, while one
breathed great draughts of the bouquet
of old brandy."

EVELYN WAUGH (1903-1966)

– ◆ –

WILLIAM RAPE

SPECIAL OCCASIONS

"Everything ends this way in France –
everything. Weddings, christenings,
duels, funerals, swindlings, diplomatic
affairs – everything is a pretext for
a good dinner."

JEAN ANOUILH (1910-1987),
from "Cécile"

– ♦ –

"Sharing food and drink is one of the oldest
rituals in the world. Whether a guest is offered a
drink by the host or a special beverage in a
special cup initiates an occasion, the moment
is of significance."

PAMELA VANDYKE PRICE

– ♦ –

"Small cheer and great welcome makes a
merry feast."

WILLIAM SHAKESPEARE (1564-1616)

– ♦ –

BONDING FAMILY AND FRIENDS

"...even those for whom cooking is an
oppressive chore or a source of self-doubting
anxiety, acknowledge that a meal shared by
friends and family is one of the bonding rituals
without which the family, society even,
can fall apart."

ANTONIA TILL,
from "Loaves & Wishes"

— ◆ —

"Dining is the privilege of civilization.... The nation which knows how to dine has learnt the leading lesson of progress."

ISABELLA BEETON (1836-1865),
from "The Book of Household Management"

— ♦ —

"Skilful and refined cookery has always been a feature of the most glorious epochs in history."

LUCIEN TENDRET

— ♦ —

"If we don't watch out, the pleasure to be gained from the discriminating enjoyment of food will be lost. It may not be long before the art of fine cooking is viewed as the invention of a handful of snobs.... A whole aspect of living well, of civilization itself, is threatened with extinction."

BENOÎTE GROULT,
from "La Mer à la Cuisine" in "Loaves & Wishes"

— ♦ —

THE KITCHEN – THE BEST ROOM

No matter where I take my guests, it seems
they like my kitchen best.

PENNSYLVANIA DUTCH SAYING

— ◆ —

"It's in the kitchen that confidences are
exchanged, that family life takes place; it's
among the remains of a meal or when you're
elbow-deep in peelings that you ask yourself
what life is all about, rather than when you're
sunk in an armchair in the sitting room."

BENOÎTE GROULT,
from "La Mer à la Cuisine" in "Loaves & Wishes"

— ◆ —

"...a friend...showed me the kitchen in her new
home with the words, 'This is my office.' I knew
what she meant. This is where I do the work I
want to, the work I like and enjoy."

SHASHI DESHPANDE

— ◆ —

THE COMFORTING KITCHEN

"From morning till night, sounds drift from the kitchen, most of them familiar and comforting.... On days when warmth is the most important need of the human heart, the kitchen is the place you can find it; it dries the wet sock, it cools the hot little brain."

E.B. WHITE (1899-1985)

– ♦ –

"In the childhood memories of every good cook, there's a large kitchen, a warm stove, a simmering pot and a mom."

BARBARA COSTIKYAN

– ♦ –

"...devote all the time and resources at your disposal to the building up of a fine kitchen. It will be, as it should be, the most comforting and comfortable room in the house."

ELIZABETH DAVID (1914-1992)